WITHDRAWN

UNITED STATES
ARMY

BY JOHN HAMILTON

VISIT US AT
WWW.ABDOPUBLISHING.COM

Published by ABDO Publishing Company, 8000 West 78th Street, Suite 310, Edina, MN 55439. Copyright ©2012 by Abdo Consulting Group, Inc. International copyrights reserved in all countries. No part of this book may be reproduced in any form without written permission from the publisher. A&D Xtreme™ is a trademark and logo of ABDO Publishing Company.

Printed in the United States of America, North Mankato, Minnesota.
042011
092011

 PRINTED ON RECYCLED PAPER

Editor: Sue Hamilton
Graphic Design: Sue Hamilton
Cover Design: John Hamilton
Cover Photo: United States Army
Interior Photos: Alamy-pgs 8 & 9; Corbis-pgs 1, 26 & 27; Thinkstock-pgs 11 & 13; United States Army-pgs 2-7, 10-25, 28-32.

Library of Congress Cataloging-in-Publication Data

Hamilton, John, 1959-
 United States Army / John Hamilton.
   p. cm. -- (United States armed forces)
 Includes index.
 ISBN 978-1-61783-069-3
 1. United States. Army--Juvenile literature. I. Title.
 UA25.H262 2012
 355.00973--dc22

                        2011012483

CONTENTS

THE UNITED STATES ARMY

The United States Army is the largest and oldest of the nation's armed forces. Its job is to preserve the nation's peace and security. The men and women of today's Army are volunteers. They freely give their time—and sometimes their lives—to defend our country.

The U.S. Army is one of the most powerful fighting forces on Earth. Its highly trained personnel can wage war anywhere in the world. The Army fights mostly on the ground, but its forces also use airplanes, helicopters, and even boats.

ARMY HISTORY

General George Washington was the Army's first commander.

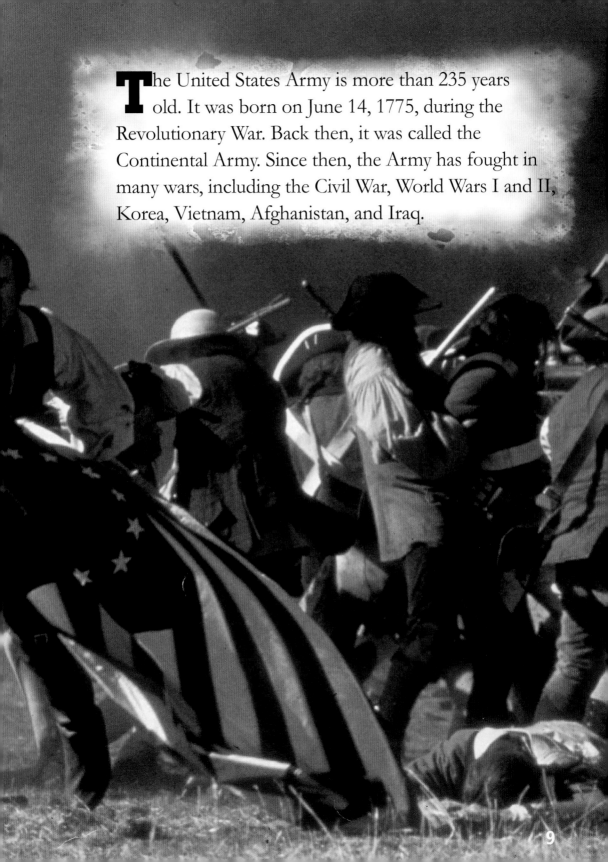

The United States Army is more than 235 years old. It was born on June 14, 1775, during the Revolutionary War. Back then, it was called the Continental Army. Since then, the Army has fought in many wars, including the Civil War, World Wars I and II, Korea, Vietnam, Afghanistan, and Iraq.

ARMY TRAINING

Army recruits must be U.S. citizens, and be at least 18 years old. Basic training lasts several weeks, at places such as Fort Benning, Georgia, and Fort Knox, Kentucky. Recruits learn combat skills, and then undergo specialty training. They become physically fit, and learn to use weapons such as assault rifles and grenades.

XTREME FACT

All recruits have nine weeks of basic training. After basic, recruits have Advanced Individual Training (AIT). In AIT they learn about their specific job in the Army. There are more than 200 jobs in the U.S. Army.

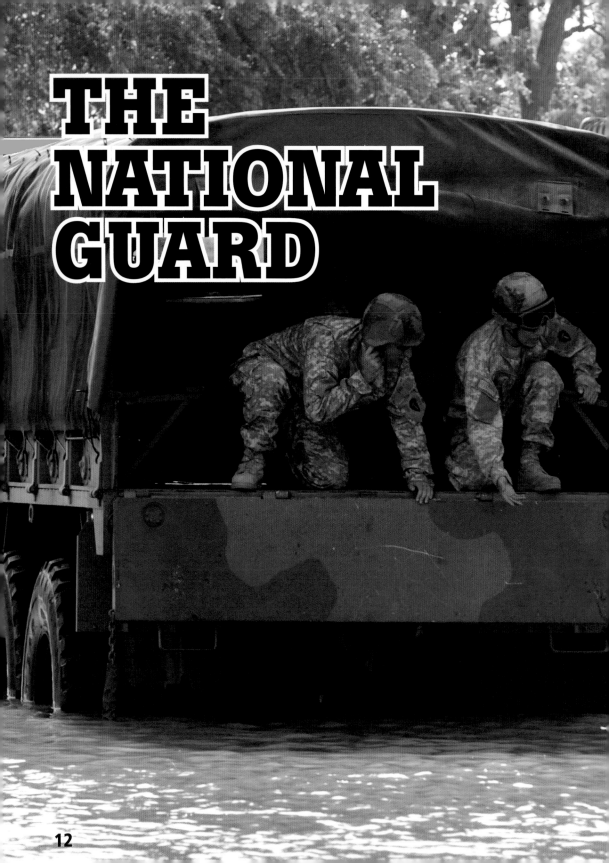

THE NATIONAL GUARD

The Army National Guard is part of the U.S. Army. It was originally made up of state militias during the Revolutionary War. Today, the Guard is commanded by individual states to help during national emergencies, such as hurricanes and earthquakes. Guard troops also fight in wars, such as Afghanistan.

INFANTRY

The backbone of the Army is the infantry. These are soldiers who fight on the ground and occupy enemy territory. Capturing land and keeping it from the enemy is the infantry's main job.

Army infantry troops are highly trained and skilled. They fight wars with assault rifles, pistols, mortars, rocket launchers, and other lethal weapons. The M16 and M4 carbine are the Army's main assault rifles. The infantry also uses radio and satellite communications to fight more effectively.

ARMORED VEHICLES

The Army uses armored vehicles to protect and transport infantry on the battlefield, and to attack the enemy. Troops can quickly be transported with vehicles such as Humvees, Strykers, and M2 Bradleys. The M1A2 is the Army's main battle tank.

XTREME FACT

The M1A2 is fast, heavily armored, and can hit far-away targets with its 120mm cannon.

ARTILLERY

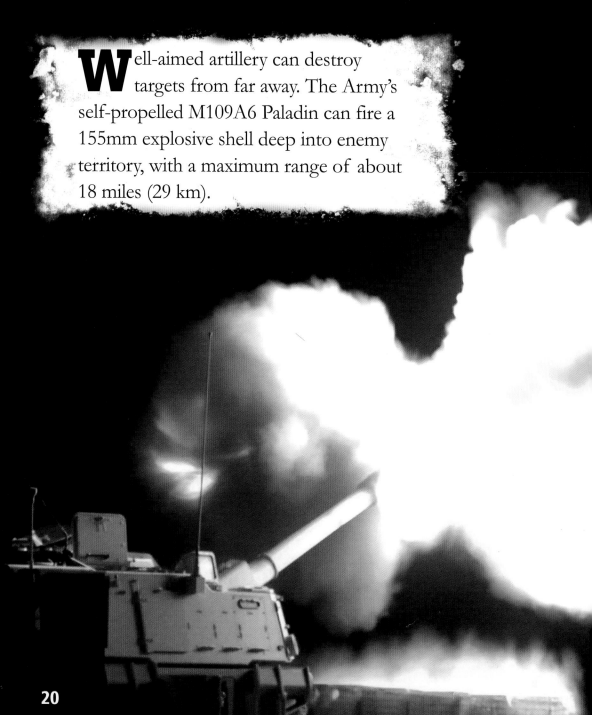

Well-aimed artillery can destroy targets from far away. The Army's self-propelled M109A6 Paladin can fire a 155mm explosive shell deep into enemy territory, with a maximum range of about 18 miles (29 km).

Loading
a shell.

Cleaning
the barrel.

HELICOPTERS

Army helicopters are often called "air cavalry." They transport soldiers and equipment to and from battlefields. They are also deadly weapons. The AH-64 Apache Longbow can easily destroy the enemy, including tanks, using machine guns and high-tech Hellfire missiles.

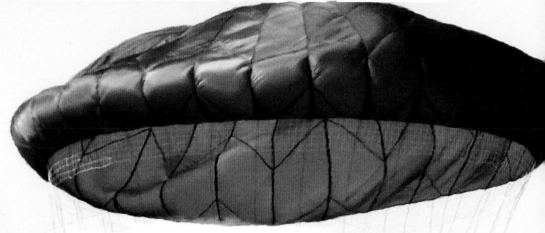

PARATROOPERS

Army paratroopers parachute into battle. Airborne soldiers and equipment can be dropped behind enemy lines. This allows them to avoid enemy strongholds on the ground. Paratroopers were used extensively during World War II. In 1989, they played a big role in the United States invasion of Panama.

A paratrooper performs a "parachute landing fall" which protects the soldier from injury.

Waves of paratroopers were used during World War II in Europe.

SPECIAL OPERATIONS

Special operations forces are highly trained for the most challenging battlefield tasks. They ambush the enemy, gather information, and conduct rescue operations. They also train our allies in foreign countries. Army special operations soldiers include Army Rangers, Green Berets, Night Stalkers, and Delta Force commandos.

XTREME FACT

Special operations soldiers may disguise themselves by wearing ghillie suits. They consist of uniforms, ponchos, or jumpsuits covered in local vegetation.

THE FUTURE

The U.S. Army is constantly changing. The global war on terrorism is a serious threat to America. Army forces are becoming lighter and quicker. Soldiers use new technology and advanced weapons systems every day. With the world's best soldiers leading the way, the U.S. Army will be able to meet whatever challenges the future holds.

A soldier models a new MultiCam Army Combat Uniform. The fire-resistant uniform provides a better camouflage pattern for soldiers in Afghanistan.

GLOSSARY

ASSAULT RIFLE

Assault rifles are the most commonly used weapons used by today's armed forces. They use medium-power cartridges (the part containing the bullet), and are fired from the shoulder. Soldiers can either fire the weapon in semiautomatic mode (one shot or short burst every time the trigger is pulled), or in fully automatic (the weapon fires rapidly until the trigger is released or ammo runs out). The U.S. Army's main assault rifles are the M16 and M4 carbine.

COMMANDO

Commandos are highly trained soldiers who specialize in raids, sometimes using techniques such as rappelling or parachuting to reach their targets. Commandos often use stealth to attack the enemy. They are also sometimes used to rescue hostages.

CONTINENTAL ARMY

The U.S. Army traces its roots to the Continental Army, which was organized by the 13 American colonies when the Revolutionary War broke out against Great Britain. Before the Continental Army was formed, each colony relied on groups of volunteers, called militias, for defense. The Second Continental Congress approved the formation of a national army on June 14, 1775. George Washington was elected to be the Continental Army's first commander in chief.

GUERRILLA WARFARE

Guerrillas are small groups of fighters (sometimes civilians instead of soldiers) who conduct quick raids or sabotage on larger armies, which are slower to respond. Guerrilla warfare uses the element of surprise to disrupt and confuse the enemy. Guerrillas often attack critical structures such as bridges or communications facilities.

MILITIA

A militia is a fighting force made of ordinary citizens who defend their territory in times of emergency. In America, before the Continental Army was formed in 1775, each colony relied on its own militia. The Minutemen were militia members. They were some of the first Americans to fight in the Revolutionary War. Militia members are usually volunteers who work without the pay of a regular army. They also have no fixed term of service, working whenever they can depending on the circumstances of an emergency. In addition to defending against invaders, militias can also provide basic law enforcement services.

MORTAR

A mortar is a portable, simple-to-use artillery weapon that launches shells (bombs) at enemies who are relatively close, within a few thousand yards. The shell is dropped into a hollow tube. When it reaches the bottom, it strikes a firing pin, which sets off a propellent, shooting the shell into the air. The shell follows a high, arching path in the sky, and then usually explodes when it hits the ground.

INDEX

DATE DUE

2-24-13	
JUN 2 8 2013	MAY – 5 2017
FEB 1 6 2014	JUL 1 3 2017
	JUL 2 1 2017
MAR – 7 2014	AUG – 7 2017
MAR 2 8 2014	
DEC – 4 2014	JUL 1 6 2018
MAY 1 1 2015	APR 2 0 2019
NOV 2 7 2015	AUG – 7 2019
JAN 1 0 2016	
NOV 3 0 2016	JUL 0 3 2022
JAN – 3 2017 FEB 2 4 2017	

PRINTED IN U.S.A.